Ayurveda C Made Easy

How To Prepare Mouth Watering Ayurveda Meals For 2 Within 30 Minutes

Introduction

Ayurveda is a system of holistic wellness and its philosophy on achieving balance is relevant today more than ever before. We live in a world where it feels like stress is the order of the day. From having to deal with traffic in the morning to having a demanding jobs to trying to balance work and a family; it almost feels like being stressed is the default. However, Ayurveda changes this by emphasizing achieving wholeness and balance through bringing balance to our Dosha

In this book, we will focus on Ayurveda cooking by looking at different foods and recipes that can bring balance to the Dosha ensuring that you achieve that holistic balance and live a more fulfilling life. Further, since I know that you are quite busy and I don't want to burden you with complicated recipes, this book has simple recipes that you can prepare in less than 30 minutes.

Table of Contents

Introduction _____ 2

Ayurveda in a Nutshell _____ 6

Understanding Doshas_____ 9

Vata Dosha _____ 9

How Vata Becomes Imbalanced _____10

Physical Symptoms of Vata Imbalanced _____ 11

How to Balance the Vata dosha _____12

Pitta Dosha _____ 21

How Pitta Dosha Becomes Imbalanced _____21

Physical Symptoms of Pitta Imbalance _____ 22

Behavioral symptoms _____ 23

How to Balance Pitta _____ 23

Kapha Dosha_____ 34

How Kapha Dosha Becomes Imbalanced _____ 34

Physical Symptoms of Kapha Imbalance _____ 35

Behavioral symptoms _____ 36

How to Balance Kapha _____ 36

Eat a Kapha-Balancing Diet_____37

Dairy/Eggs: _____ 41

Breakfast _____ 45

Breakfast Kitchari _____ 45

Tasty Oatmeal _____ 48

Sweet Potato Porridge_____ 50

Breakfast Buckwheat _____ 54

Ojas-Increasing Oatmeal _____ 58

Low Carb Flat-bread_____ 61

Bhat Bhaja _____ 63

Main Meals _____ 66

Instant Pot Dal Fry _____ 66

Sweet Potato with Kale _____ 69

Instant Pot Aloo Matar _____ 71

Coconut and Kale Sauté_____ 74

Cauliflower Steak with Chickpea Salad_____ 78

Snacks and Side Dishes _____ 80

Summertime Salad _____ 80

Sweet Lassi _____ 83

Coconut Curry Hummus _____ 86

Steamed Veggies _____ 89

Kale Chips _____ 92

Beverages _____ 95

Cucumber Coconut Juice _____ 95

Super Greens Smoothie _____ 97

Turmeric Milkshake _____ 99

Detox Soup _____ 101

Vata-Reducing Smoothie _____ 103

Rice Drink _____ 106

Avocado Shake _____ 108

Conclusion _____ 110

Ayurveda in a Nutshell

Let us start by first understanding what Ayurveda means. The term "Ayurveda" is a system of medicine that has roots in India. Ayurveda simply translates to "science of life" or just "knowledge of life."

The core principle of Ayurvedic practice is based on the belief that health and wellness ultimately depend on the perfect balance between the body, mind, and spirit. As a form of medicine and lifestyle approach, Ayurveda generally focuses on your health and wellness and incorporates various beliefs and practices that bring about significant benefits. One main Ayurvedic belief is that a majority of diseases often start in the digestive tract; therefore, the food you eat is your very first "medicine" for most diseases!

Some of the benefits you can enjoy by adopting Ayurvedic medicine and lifestyle practices include:

Weight Loss

Ayurvedic practices are a form of alternative medicine that can help you shed off stubborn body fat. For instance, herbs associated with Ayurveda, such as guggul and Triphala, have been linked to improved weight loss. In addition, exercises and body movements in yoga classes combined with mindful eating, can go a long way in promoting weight loss.

Reduced Inflammation

Generally, inflammatory reactions are caused by various problems such as an unhealthy diet, digestive disorders, some drugs, or other underlying health issues. Ayurveda focuses on diet, mindfulness, sleep, and exercising all that have the potential to lower inflammatory reactions by eliminating underlying problems. Also, a study that was conducted showed that ayurvedic herbs such as turmeric have a significant impact in reducing inflammation; and can help address conditions such as anxiety, arthritis, metabolic syndrome and hyperlipidemia.

Improved Heart Health

A scientific study found out that ayurvedic medicine does have a positive effect, particularly with patients suffering from coronary heart disease. The study concluded that Ayurveda practices such as meditation and yoga have shown to help in controlling blood pressure.

Boosts Sleep

Lack of sleep or poor-quality sleep is linked to dietary ingredients, among them, alcohol, caffeine, and processed foods. Ayurvedic practices are more balanced approaches that emphasize mindfulness and healthy eating to help improve sleep. Furthermore, Ayurvedic based oils such as coconut or jasmine once massaged on your temples do have a relaxing effect that enables you to get a good night's rest.

One other major belief in Ayurveda is that everything in our universe is composed of 5 elements, which are water, air, fire, earth, and space. Ayurveda mainly operates on the *qualities* and *powers* of these major elements. Therefore, the importance of keeping these five basic elements balanced to have a healthy body, mind, and spirit, which brings us to how these elements control something referred to as *dosha*. Let us learn more about doshas in the following chapter.

Understanding Doshas

Doshas are the biological energies that are found in the human body and mind that control all the physical and emotional processes. It is critical to note that each individual is governed by various elements more than other people depending on their natural constitution, which is referred to as *dosha*.

There are three types of doshas:

- Kapha dosha - where water and earth elements are dominant

- Vata dosha - where space and air elements are dominant

- Pitta dosha - where the fire element is dominant

Let's get to understand what these dosha types entail and how they affect you:

Vata Dosha

Dominated by air and space elements, Vata dosha is all about the energy of unrestricted movement, and for this reason, Vata is associated with the *wind*. The main locations of Vata in your body are the brain, skin, joints, bones, thighs, colon, ears, and nerve tissues. Psychologically, Vata is linked to the quickness of thought, communication, creativity, flexibility, and a free-flowing spirit. Physiologically, Vata is associated with bodily movements among them talking, breathing, nerve impulses, blood circulation, and muscle contraction.

If your dominant dosha is Vata, you're likely to be physically and mentally active and may like traveling to unknown territories, meeting new friends, and enjoying other creative endeavors. You are also like to be slender, with dry skin, feel cold often and often experience racing thoughts. Any **imbalance** in Vata dosha will result in digestive problems such as constipation along with emotional instability such as fear and anxiety.

How Vata Becomes Imbalanced

- Drinking black tea, coffee, and alcohol

- Smoking cigarettes

- Getting to bed late at night

- Adopting an irregular daily routine

- Eating while on the run

- Eating food while feeling depressed or anxious

- Eating Vata-provoking foods such as cold and dehydrating foods

Vata dosha is the most significant of the 3 doshas since its imbalance goes for a very long time and can ultimately upset the other two doshas. Here are the symptoms you're likely to experience if you're Vata imbalanced:

Physical Symptoms of Vata Imbalanced

- Dry and rough skin

- Dehydration

- Tremors and twitches

- Constipation

- Lack of sleep or disturbed sleep

- Pain and body-aches such as cramps, joint pain

- Increased sensitivity to cold

- Loss of strength and increased fatigue

- Feeling dizzy

- Astringent taste in your mouth

- Distension or gas formation in the abdomen

- Weight loss

- Dryness, scaling

- Weakening of muscles

Behavioral symptoms

- Excessive talking or uncontrollable movement

- Feeling ungrounded

- Feeling fearful confused and shaky

- Wanting to run away

- Feeling anxious, nervous and agitated

- Being impatient

- Phobias

- Convulsion, tremors and panic attacks

How to Balance the Vata dosha

You will need to practice anything that brings about grounding and stability, such as meditation with your feet on earth or other adjustments to your lifestyle. Here's what you can do:

- Doing daily meditation

- Going to bed early

- Adopt a regular day to day routine

- Dining in a quiet and peaceful environment

- Doing physical exercises such as swimming, yoga or just having a walk

Eating a Vata Friendly Diet

Vata balancing foods are mostly high in fats and proteins, along with warmth generating foods. Thus you should experiment with a variety of meats, warm creamy drinks, and root vegetables. It is recommendable to be well hydrated to combat symptoms of dehydration and skin dryness. Here is the complete list of foods to eat and avoid:

Foods To Eat And Avoid In Vata

Vegetables (cooked)

Eat-in plenty

- Garlic

- Cucumber

- Turnips

- Radishes

- Sweet potatoes

- Carrots

- Beets

- Onions

- Green beans

- Asparagus

Eat-in moderation (cooked)

- Mushrooms

- Leafy green vegetables

- Eggplant

- Zucchini

- Peas

- Celery

- Tomatoes

- Sprouts

- Potatoes

- Cabbage

- Brussels sprouts

- Peppers

- Cauliflower

- Broccoli

Avoid

Do not eat raw veggies

Fruits (well ripened)

- Pineapple

- Cherries

- Plums

- Berries

- Sour oranges

- Peaches

- Mangoes

- Stewed fruits

- Papaya

- Bananas

- Grapefruit

- Sweet melons

- Apricots

- Grapes

- Lemons

- Avocados

- Fresh figs

- Coconut

Fruits to eat in moderation

- Pomegranates

- Pears

- Cranberries

Fruits To avoid

- All unripe fruit

- All dried fruits

Grains

- Cooked rice

- Oats, particularly cooked oatmeal cereal

Grains to eat in moderation

- Buckwheat

- Millet

- Dry oat

- Corn

- Barley

- Wheat

Dairy

You can take any dairy and its related products.

Meat

- Turkey

- Seafood

- Chicken

In moderation

- Red meat

Beans

- Pink lentils

- Mung beans

- Chickpeas

Beans in moderation

- Black beans

- Kidney beans

Cooking oils

- Olive oil

- Ghee

- Sesame oil

Sweeteners, nuts, and seeds

All sweeteners, seeds, and nuts are generally acceptable if consumed in small amounts.

Herbs & Spices

- Turmeric

- Saffron

To avoid

- Thyme

- Parsley

- Fenugreek

- Coriander seed

Pitta Dosha

This dosha type is linked to fire and therefore is perceived as very strong, intense, and often irritable. Pitta dosha is believed to govern the digestive, metabolic, and endocrine body systems. Thus, when the pitta dosha is dominant in you, you may seem busy, competitive, always on the go, and a high achiever. You are also likely to be a quick learner and natural leader whose skills in adopting new concepts make you impatient and judgmental about other people who tend to be docile. You also tend to have strong digestion and a high appetite for food and might even become grumpy after missing a meal. This makes Pitta dosha more prone o inflammation, loss stool, acne, rashes, and you feel cool often.

How Pitta Dosha Becomes Imbalanced

- Smoking cigarettes

- Being overly competitive

- Overworking

- Eating while angry

- Drinking coffee, alcohol or black tea

- Eating Pitta-provoking food particularly **hot, spicy, or fermented foods**

Physical Symptoms of Pitta Imbalance

- Nausea and headache

- Loose bowel movements or excess eliminations

- Bitter taste in the mouth

- Strong body odor

- Skin rashes, pimples, and boils

- Hypertension

- Bleeding

- Heartburn and acidity

- Inflammations

- Sensitiveness to heat and bright light

- Hot flashes and burning sensations in hands and soles of feet

- Vomiting yellowish water, the bile

- Excessive thirst or hunger

Behavioral symptoms

- Frustration

- Impatience and restlessness

- Aggressive attitude

- Anger, hostility, and irritability

- Criticizing tendencies and being judgmental

- Hyperactivity in speech and actions

How to Balance Pitta

- Avoid artificial stimulants

- Practice daily meditation

- Loosening your tight schedule

- Spending some time in nature

- Eating in a restful environment

- Doing relaxing exercises such as walking, swimming or yoga

Eating a Pitta-balancing diet

You should focus on cooling foods and drinks such as grains, coconut water, and sweet fruits.

Here is the full food list:

Vegetables

- Spinach

- Carrot

- Zucchini

- Mushrooms

- Leafy green vegetables

- Sweet potatoes

- Squash

- Green beans

- Okra

- Lettuce

- Cabbage

- Sprouts

- Potatoes

- Asparagus

- Peas

- Brussels sprouts

- Parsley

- Green (sweet) peppers

- Cucumber

- Broccoli

- Celery

- Radishes

- Cauliflower

In moderation

- Beets

- Chilies

- Hot peppers

Ayurveda Cooking Made Easy

- Tomatoes

- Onion

- Eggplant

Fruits

- Raisins

- Prunes

- Avocados

- Plums

- Melons

- Pineapples

- Bananas

- Oranges

- Pears

- Mangoes

- Figs

- Cherries

In moderation

- Dark grapes

- Raw papaya

- Pineapples

- Grapefruit

- Berries

- Apricot

- Persimmon

- Sour cherries

- Apples

- Peaches

Fruits to Avoid

- Plum

- Pineapple

- Oranges

Ensure that all fruits are sweet

Grains

- White rice

- Barley

- Wheat

- Oats

In moderation:

- Millet

- Corn

- Rye

- Brown rice

Dairy and Eggs

- Milk

- Clarified butter or ghee

- Fruit sorbets (shouldn't be sour)

- Egg whites

- Butter

In moderation:

- Sour cream

- Egg yolk

- Sour buttermilk

- Cheese

- Ice cream

- Sour yogurt

Meats

- River fish

- Turkey

- Shrimp

- Chicken

In moderation:

- Most seafood

- Red meat

Legumes

- Tofu

- Red lentils

- Mung beans

- Chickpeas

- Soybean products (fresh, not fermented)

In moderation

- Black lentils

- Black gram

Best Oils

- Grape-seed oil

- Sunflower oil

- Soy oil

- Olive oil

In moderation

- Coconut oil

- Safflower oil

- Almond oil

- Sesame oil

- Corn oil

Nuts & Seeds

- Flax-seeds

- Pumpkin seeds

- Coconut

- Sunflower seeds

Sweeteners

Most organic sweeteners are acceptable

Avoid

- Molasses

- Honey

Herbs and Spices

In moderation

- Black pepper

- Cumin

- Turmeric

- Saffron

- Mint

- Cardamom

- Fennel

- Dill

- Coriander seed

- Cinnamon

- Green coriander (cilantro)

Note

You should avoid using too much spice since most are too hot for a Pitta dosha type.

Kapha Dosha

Linked to earth and water, Kapha dosha is stabilizing energy that is believed to supply water to your body and stimulate the immune system. These attributes make people wit dominant Kapha dosha naturally athletic as they need regular exercises to control their tendency to gain bodyweight. The association of earth and water also makes Kapha types calm, stable, compassionate, loyal, and forgiving. They also like to carry out activities in an organized step by step approach and always follow a particular fixed personal and professional routine. Compared to Vata or Pitta dosha, they tend to have reduced appetite and slowed metabolism. Therefore, people with dominant Kapha dosha are likely to benefit from occasional fasting.

Any imbalance in Kapha can bring problems such as weight gain, sluggishness, and jealousy, among others. Here are ways in which such an imbalance can happen:

How Kapha Dosha Becomes Imbalanced

- Overeating

- Avoiding physical activity

- Not engaging in intellectual challenges

- Staying most of the time indoors

- Staying in very cold and damp environments for long

- Eating sweet foods to control bad emotions particularly when depressed

- Eating Kapha-provoking foods such as **sugary, heavy and dense foods**

Physical Symptoms of Kapha Imbalance

- Excessive sleep

- Lethargy

- Weight gain

- Water retention and swelling

- Congestion, excess mucus formation

- Depression

- Difficulty in breathing

- Loss of appetite

- Nausea and indigestion

Behavioral symptoms

- Dull, laziness

- Depression, stress or sadness

- Feeling greedy or possessive

- Feeling lonely, lack of support or unloved

- Feeling of heaviness

How to Balance Kapha

- Engaging in plenty of exercises

- Doing mindful activities like meditation and deep breathing

- Doing housekeeping regularly

- Going to bed early and waking up early

- Avoiding or significantly reducing daytime naps

- Eating in a love rich environment

- Practicing non-attachment in daily life

- Differentiating between being nice and "being taken advantage of"

- Slowing down on luxurious or leisurely lifestyle

Eat a Kapha-Balancing Diet

The key is to avoid those heavy, dense, and oily foods, among them rice and pasta, and instead overindulge in plenty of vegetables and fruits.

Here is the recommended diet in details:

Vegetables

- Spinach

- Mushrooms

- Broccoli

- Cauliflower

- Potatoes

- Sprouts

- Asparagus

- Radishes

- Cabbage

- Onions

- Leafy green vegetables

- Beets

- Okra

- Celery

- Pea's peppers

- Lettuce

- Garlic

- Carrots

- Eggplant

- Brussels sprouts

In moderation:

- Sweet potatoes

- Zucchini

- Tomatoes

- Cucumbers

Fruits

- Grapefruit
- Papaya
- Apples
- Cherries
- Prunes
- Berries
- Pomegranates
- Apricots
- Pears
- Cranberries

Dried fruits

- Prunes
- Figs
- Apricots

- Raisins

In moderation:

- Coconuts

- Bananas

- Fresh figs

- Dates

- Mangoes

Grains

- Basmati rice

- Buckwheat

- Rye

- Oats

- Millet

- Corn

- Barley

In moderation:

- Wheat

- Rice

To avoid

- Steamed grains

- Hot cereals

Dairy/Eggs:

- Goat's milk

- Boiled eggs (or not cooked with butter)

- Whole milk

- Warm skim milk

- Camel milk

In moderation:

- Egg yolks

Meats

- Lean fish

- Small amounts of turkey

- Chicken

In moderation

- Red meat

- Shrimp

Legumes

Most legumes are acceptable.

In moderation:

- Tofu

- Kidney beans

Oils

- Olive oil

- Sunflower oil

Ayurveda Cooking Made Easy

- Almond oil

- Grape-seed oil (all in little quantities)

Sweeteners

You can use most of them but in very small quantities.

Nuts & Seeds

- Flax seeds

- Pumpkin seeds

- Sunflower seeds

Herbs & Spices

- Ginger

- Sesame

- Fenugreek

- Cumin

- Most of the spices are okay, particularly those that boost digestion.

With that information, perhaps it's much easier to decide your meal plan depending on what dosha is dominant for you. Let us now look at amazing recipes that you can prepare to balance various doshas.

Breakfast

Breakfast Kitchari

Dosha Effect: Suitable in helping reduce Kapha, and Vata and balance Pitta

Prep Time: 5 minutes

Cook Time: 25 minutes

Total Time: 30 minutes

Serves: 2

Ingredients

½ teaspoon ghee

1 1/2 tablespoons coconut, shredded

2 to 4 teaspoons honey (or maple syrup for Pitta)

2 tablespoons cashew pieces

4 dates, pitted and chopped (or 2 dates for Kapha)

1/2 cup grated carrots

1/2 cup basmati rice

1 cinnamon stick

¼ teaspoon cumin seeds

1 tablespoon sesame oil (for pitta use coconut oil)

2/3 cup mung dal

3 cups water

Large pinch salt

Coconut, for garnish

Cinnamon, for garnish

1-1/2 teaspoons Ayurvedic spices OR

1/4 teaspoon cardamom powder

1/2 teaspoon ginger powder

1 teaspoon cinnamon

1/2 teaspoon turmeric

Directions

1. Add water to a medium sized pan and bring it to a boil. Once the water begins to boil, lower the heat to low.

2. Stir in cinnamon stick, mung dal, and a sufficient amount of salt. Now cover the pan but leave a little crack to prevent any overflow.

3. Cook for approximately 15 minutes, stirring after about 7 or 8 minutes. Meanwhile, start grating the carrot.

4. Add in the grated carrots along with the basmati rice, and stir well until incorporated. Then replace the lid and cook for another 15 minutes, while stirring at 5 minutes intervals.

5. Lower the heat to low and then add in ghee, coconut, cashew pieces, chopped dates and the breakfast spices.

6. Switch off the heat leaving the pan on the burner. Cover the saucepan fully and allow it sit for about 5 minutes.

7. Serve the kitchari into 2 bowls and let it cool down. Add in about 1 or 2 teaspoons of honey per each bowl and sprinkle with a little coconut and cinnamon.

8. Consider replacing the basmati rice with millet and quinoa if you are a Kapha type as these are unrefined, lighter, healthy and with higher nutritional value.

Tasty Oatmeal

Dosha Effect: Tridoshic, suitable for Vata, Pitta and Kapha

Prep Time: 5 minutes

Cook Time: 20 minutes

Total Time: 25 minutes

Serves 2

Ingredients

1-2 tablespoons pumpkin seeds

1/2 teaspoon ground turmeric

1/8 teaspoon ground cloves or/and 1/4 teaspoon ground cardamom

2 cinnamon sticks

300 ml soy or any other vegan milk

80 grams oatmeal flakes

1-2 tablespoons raisins

200 grams (1 cup) pumpkin flesh, cut in bite-size cubes

200 ml water

Directions

1. First, cover the raisins and pumpkin with some water and bring the mixture to a boil.

2. Cook on low heat for approximately 10 minutes.

3. Add in soymilk or other vegan nondairy milk and bring the mixture to a boil.

4. Add in turmeric, cardamom powder, cinnamon sticks and oatmeal flakes and cook for additional 10 minutes.

5. Sprinkle the oatmeal with some pumpkin seeds and then enjoy.

Sweet Potato Porridge

Dosha Effect: Reduces Kapha, Vata and Pitta imbalance. Check notes below.

Prep Time: 5 minutes

Cook Time: 25 minutes

Total Time: 30 minutes

Serves: 2

Ingredients

2-6 teaspoons honey, divided

Splash almond milk

1 tablespoon shredded coconut

1 teaspoon ghee

1 cup chopped sweet potato

2 cinnamon sticks

3/4 cup millet

2 cups almond milk or whole milk, divided

3 cups water

Shredded coconut for garnish

Cinnamon, for garnish

1 1/2 teaspoons Ayurvedic Breakfast Spices or

1/8 teaspoon cardamom powder

1/8 teaspoon turmeric

1/2 teaspoon ginger powder

1 teaspoon cinnamon

Directions

1. Put almond milk and water in a medium pan over high heat and bring the mixture to a boil.

2. Meanwhile, begin chopping the sweet potato into 1/2 to 1/4 inch small cubes.

3. Lower the heat to medium low setting and add in cinnamon sticks, sweet potato and the millet.

4. Cook while uncovered for approximately 20 minutes, while stirring at 5 minutes intervals.

5. Check how the porridge is. In case it is somehow dry, add in a tablespoon of almond milk or water, and cook it while

covered for at least 1 minute as you stir every additional minute. If need be, add in more liquid.

6. As soon as the millet is soft, switch off the heat but leave the saucepan on the burner.

7. Add in coconut, ghee and the spices. Cover the pan and allow the porridge to sit for another 4 to 5 minutes so as the porridge can soften and the flavors blend.

8. Serve the porridge into bowls, and then add approximately 1 to 3 teaspoons of honey to each bowl.

9. Top with a dash of almond milk and cinnamon if you want along with coconut.

10. Serve the porridge and enjoy.

Doshic Recommendations

For Vata:

As millet is somewhat dry and lighter in quality, you may need to increase grounding. Also consider increasing coconut to 2 tablespoons and ghee to 2 teaspoons. You can add more sweet potato if required though this will require more cooking time.

For Pitta:

Millet might be a little hot for you so consider adding cooling ingredients. You may also double the amounts of coconut and ghee. Replace honey with maple syrup and garnish the porridge with shredded coconut. (not additional cinnamon).

For Kapha:

Millet is okay for you since it's dry, warming, light and crunchy. Consider replacing dairy milk with almond milk instead. Omit the ghee and use 2-3 teaspoons of ground flax seeds in place of coconut. Increase the breakfast spices to 2 teaspoons to improve digestion.

Ayurveda Cooking Made Easy

Breakfast Buckwheat

Dosha Effect: Tri-doshic, it helps reduce Kapha, Vata and Pitta imbalance

Prep Time: 5 minutes

Cook Time: 25 minutes

Total Time: 30 minutes

Serves: 2

Ingredients

1 teaspoon ghee

2 teaspoons coconut, shredded

30 raisins

1/2 teaspoon ginger

1/4 teaspoon cardamom

1 teaspoon ashwagandha, if needed

1 teaspoon cinnamon

1/2 teaspoon turmeric

1 cup almond milk, unsweetened

Pinch salt

1 cup raw buckwheat groats

2 cups water

2 to 4 teaspoons honey

Splash almond milk

Cinnamon, for garnish

Directions

1. In a small saucepan add in some water and then bring it to a boil. Once fully boiling, lower the heat to low and stir in a pinch of salt and buckwheat groats. Cover the pan, but leave a slight opening to prevent overflow. Cook until the buckwheat is plumped up and the liquid has dried up, or for approximately 15 minutes. Keep stirring after each 5 minutes or so.

2. Stir in ghee, coconut, raisins, ginger, cardamom, ashwagandha, cinnamon, turmeric and almond milk while stirring now and again.

3. Cook the mixture until the buckwheat is soft enough, or for another 2 to 3 minutes.

4. Serve the buckwheat into 2 bowls, and top individual bowls with some cinnamon and almond milk.

5. As soon as the groats have somehow cooled down, add in 1 to 2 teaspoons of honey in each bowl.

6. Serve the buckwheat as light breakfast for all dosha types.

Doshic Variations

For Vata:

Instead of 1 cup of buckwheat, consider blending 1/2 cup of steel cut oats together with 1/2 cup of buckwheat instead to add extra heartiness. You can add more shredded coconut and ghee to get more benefits.

For Pitta:

Replace honey with maple syrup and ashwagandha with shatavari powder as these ingredients could be too heating for you.

Kapha:

If at Kapha imbalance, omit or reduce the quantities of shredded coconut, salt, raisins and ghee. Reduce the amount of almond milk or replace it with water. Consider adding more spices to boost metabolism.

Ayurveda Cooking Made Easy

Ojas-Increasing Oatmeal

Dosha Effect: Reduces Vata and Pitta imbalance. Increases Kapha; see notes to make it more suitable for Kapha

Prep Time: 10 minutes

Cook Time: 25 minutes

Total Time: 35 minutes

Serves: 2

Ingredients

1 to 2 tablespoons honey or maple syrup for Pitta

2 teaspoons ghee

1 teaspoon vanilla extract

1/2 teaspoon ginger powder*

1/4 teaspoon cardamom powder*

1 1/2 teaspoons cinnamon powder*

1 tablespoon almond butter

2 tablespoons shredded coconut

2 pitted and chopped medjool dates

20 raisins

1/8 teaspoon salt

1 cup steel cut oats

3.25 cups water

Coconut, for garnish

Dash cinnamon, for garish

Note

*You can replace the starred spices with 1 teaspoon of the Ayurvedic Breakfast Spices.

Directions

1. Into a medium saucepan, add in some water and then bring it to a boil. Once boiling, lower the heat.

2. Add in some salt along with the steel cut oats. Cook the mixture on low medium heat while covered, for approximately 20 minutes, while stirring after each 7 to 10 minutes.

3. Switch off the heat but leave the pan on the burner. Add in ghee, vanilla, ginger, cardamom, cinnamon, almond butter, coconut, chopped dates and raisins.

4. Stir until all ingredients are incorporated. Cover the saucepan with a lid for about 5 minutes to soften the oats.

5. Serve the oatmeal in bowls, and then let it cool for a moment. Add in a sprinkle of coconut, a dash of cinnamon and 1 to 3 tablespoons of honey if you like.

6. Serve and enjoy.

Doshic Variations

Pitta:

Consider replacing honey with maple syrup; though this is very optional.

For Kapha:

Replace the steel cut oats with equal amount of buckwheat groats. Also use 1 tablespoon of grounded flax seed in place of shredded coconut and omit the almond butter and dates altogether. You can double the amounts of spices if you want.

Low Carb Flat-bread

Dosha Effect: Suitable for Vata

Prep Time: 5 minutes

Cook Time: 12 minutes

Total Time: 17 minutes

Serves: 2

Ingredients

1/2 cup boiling water

1 teaspoon beef gelatin in 1 tablespoon boiling water

1 1/2 tablespoons coconut oil or ghee

1/8 teaspoon salt

1/8 teaspoon baking powder

1/2 tablespoon psyllium husk powder

3 tablespoons coconut flour

Directions

1. In a medium bowl, whisk together coconut flour, psyllium husk powder, baking powder, and salt until incorporated.

2. Beat in ghee, boiling water and dissolved gelatin until you get firm dough.

3. Divide the dough into two balls and flatten them in between plastic wrap or parchment paper into 5-inch circles.

3. Heat a non-stick skillet over medium-high heat, and then add in some ghee. Heat until melted and then add a dough circle. Lower the heat to medium.

4. Cook the flat bread for approximately 12 minutes or until golden on both sides; while flipping as required.

5. Repeat for the other flat breads and then serve warm.

Notes

The cooking oils and animal products used in this recipe are Vata friendly.

Bhat Bhaja

Dosha Effect: Balances Pitta and Vata

Prep Time: 15 minutes

Cook Time: 10 minutes

Total Time: 25 minutes

Serves 2

Ingredients

3-4 pods green cardamom

4-5 cloves

1 inch cinnamon stick

1 tablespoon ghee

1.5 tablespoons oil

Sugar, to taste

Salt, to taste

1 teaspoon black pepper powder

1/2 teaspoon coriander powder

1/2 teaspoon cumin powder

2 green chilli chopped

2 onions chopped

2 eggs

4 cups plain rice cooked/left over rice

A handful coriander leaves, chopped (skip for Vata)

Directions

1. Add oil in a pan, heat it and then add some ghee. Allow the ghee to melt fully.

2. Temper the ghee with green cardamom pods, cloves and cinnamon sticks.

3. Allow the ingredients to crackle and develop some fragrance. Add in chopped onion and the green chili and then cook until the color changes.

4. Add in a little sugar, salt, coriander powder and cumin and combine well.

5. Now, add in the rice and mix it carefully.

6. Crack open the eggs in a separate bowl and add some salt. Beat eggs well.

Ayurveda Cooking Made Easy

7. Add the egg mixture in the karai and watch as the egg coats the rice and forms a scramble-like texture.

8. Then add in the black pepper and mix well. Take care when mixing; do it gently as the rice might turn mushy and alter the flavor and taste.

9. Now, add in the chopped coriander leaves and combine well.

10. Sauté the bhat bhaja for another 2 minutes and then serve it hot!

Main Meals

Instant Pot Dal Fry

Dosha Effect: Suitable for Vata and Pitta

Prep Time: 10 minutes

Cook Time: 15 minutes

Total Time: 15 minutes

Serves: 2

Ingredients

2 tablespoons coriander leaves, chopped

1 teaspoon lemon juice

½ teaspoon dried fenugreek leaves

½ teaspoon Gram masala

2 ¼ cups water

Salt to taste

1 teaspoon coriander powder

1 teaspoon red chili powder

½ teaspoon turmeric powder

½ cup tomato chopped finely

1 teaspoon freshly grated garlic

1 green chili chopped finely

½ cup onion chopped

2 tablespoons oil

2 tablespoons masoor dal

2 tablespoons split and skinless yellow moong dal

¼ cup split pigeon peas

Directions

1. Wash the dals and then soak them for around 15 minutes.

2. Press on the sauté button then add oil and cumin seeds to the hot cooking pot. Allow the seeds to sizzle.

3. Then add in onions and let them cook for about 1 or 2 minutes. Mix the green chili and garlic paste and cook for 40 to 50 seconds or so.

4. As soon as the raw smell goes away, add in tomatoes and let them cook until soft or for about 2 minutes.

5. Then add in turmeric powder, salt, coriander powder and salt, and mix.

6. At this point, add the soaked dal along with water and stir to incorporate. Cover the instant pot and set it to Venting.

7. Set the timer to 5 minutes if already soaked or for 7 minutes if you had not soaked the dal.

8. Naturally pressure release for around 5 minutes then do a quick release. Carefully open the lid and stir the mixture.

9. Check if extra water is required and if so add some water. Turn back to sauté and cook for a few seconds.

10. Then mix in lemon juice, kasoori methi and garam masala. Garnish the dish with coriander leaves and enjoy.

Notes

While high amount of spices are advisable for Kapha for boosting digestion, it is good to replace turmeric with Kapha Churna.

Sweet Potato with Kale

Dosha Effect: Suitable for Pitta

Prep Time: 10 minutes

Cook Time: 15 minutes

Total Time: 25 minutes

Serves: 2

Ingredients

2 cups sweet potato

1 tablespoons sunflower oil

2 pinch salt (mineral salt)

½ lb. kale

¾-inch fresh ginger

Directions

1. Boil the kale leaves until they achieve a vibrant shade of green and become stained.

2. Add in the diced sweet potatoes in another pot and cover with enough water until well covered.

Ayurveda Cooking Made Easy

3. Season with some salt and boil until softened. Then remove the kale and sweet potatoes and reserve the cooking liquid for another recipe.

4. Now grate and sauté the ginger in a little sunflower oil for about 30 minutes. Then add the cooked kale and sweet potatoes.

5. Combine the ginger carefully so as not to break the sweet potatoes.

Instant Pot Aloo Matar

Dosha Effect: Suitable for Kapha

Prep Time: 10 minutes

Cook Time: 5 minutes

Total Time: 15 minutes

Serves 2

Ingredients

2 cup potatoes peeled and cubed

1 cup green peas

2 tablespoons coriander leaves, chopped

1 teaspoon fenugreek seeds, ground

½ teaspoon garam masala

1 cup water

Salt

1 teaspoon cumin powder

1 teaspoon coriander powder

½ teaspoon turmeric powder

1 ½ teaspoons crushed ginger

1 green chili finely chopped

1 cup tomato chopped

1 ½ teaspoons red chili powder

1 teaspoon cumin seeds

2 tablespoons oil

Directions

1. Press on the sauté function then add in oil. Add cumin seeds to the hot cooking pot and allow them sizzle for a moment.

2. Then add in green chili, ginger, tomatoes and cook until the tomatoes are soft. Turn off the sauté mode by pressing the cancel button.

3. Now, mix in cumin powder, coriander powder, red chili powder, turmeric powder and salt.

4. Add in peas, potato cubes and water. Cover and set the instant pot to Sealing.

5. Set cooking time to 4 minutes on Manual mode and cook at high pressure. Once done, quick release and open the lid.

6. Now, add in kasoori methi and garam masala. Then use a spatula to mix in mashed potatoes to thicken the gravy.

7. Garnish the aloo matar with chopped coriander leaves.

Notes

If need be, consider replacing the turmeric with Kapha Churna (optional).

Coconut and Kale Sauté

Dosha Effect: Reduces Pitta and Kapha imbalance. It also increases Vata. See the notes to make it more Vata-friendly.

Prep Time: 5 minutes

Cook Time: 10 minutes

Total Time: 15 minutes

Serves: 2 to 3

Ingredients

1/8 teaspoon salt

1/2 lime, juiced

2 tablespoons coconut, shredded

1/4 cup water

1 tablespoon finely minced fresh ginger

1 tablespoon almond slivers

1/2 teaspoon cumin seed, whole

1 tablespoon coconut oil

1 bunch of kale

1 teaspoon Pitta Churna *or a mixture of*

1 teaspoon ginger powder

1 pinch of cardamom

1/4 teaspoon fennel powder

1/4 teaspoon coriander powder

1/4 teaspoon cumin powder

1/4 teaspoon turmeric

Directions

1. First, cut off the stem from the kale and then chop the kale leaves into thin slices.

2. Heat a large pan over medium heat. Once hot, add in coconut oil.

3. As soon as it is heated through, add in the slivered almonds and cumin seeds and sauté for approximately 2 minutes while stirring often.

4. Add in fresh ginger and Pitta masala and sauté for an additional 30 seconds. In case you cannot get Pitta masala, just add 1/4 teaspoon of each coriander, cumin, fennel and turmeric.

5. Add in water and chopped kale and stir well until the kale is evenly coated with the spice and oil.

6. Cook over medium heat for approximately 4 minutes while stirring constantly.

7. Now stir in the shredded coconut and cook for another 30 seconds. Switch off the heat while leaving the pan on the burner.

8. Add in some salt and lime juice and blend until everything is well incorporated.

Doshic Variations

Vata:

You might find kale provoking in that it is airy, rough and dry. So to cook the kale, add 4 tablespoons of water and cook for approximately 5 minutes while stirring at 30 to 60 seconds intervals. Add extra water if needed to help add extra moisture and make it more digestible. Replace coconut oil with 2 tablespoons of sesame oil and use lemon in place of lime juice as lemon is warming and reduces Vata.

Kapha:

Cut down the amounts of almonds and coconut in half if too heavy for you. Also you can use sunflower oil in place of coconut oil and use more spices to boost digestion. Use Kapha Churna in place of Pitta Churna.

Ayurveda Cooking Made Easy

Cauliflower Steak with Chickpea Salad

Dosha Effect: Balances Vata

Prep Time: 10 minutes

Cook time: 18 minutes

Total Time: 28 minutes

Serves 2

Ingredients

50g feta cheese, crumbled

4 red finely sliced radishes

125g cooked chickpeas

2 vine tomatoes, chopped

¼ small finely sliced red onion

3 tablespoons tandoori paste

1 whole cauliflower

Large handful fresh coriander, chopped

For the dressing

1 tablespoon water

1 tablespoon crème fraîche

Coriander chutney

Directions

1. Preheat your oven to about 200 degrees Celsius.

2. Meanwhile, start making the dressing. Just mix all the ingredients for the dressing and set the mixture aside.

3. Begin slicing the cauliflower into steak shaped pieces and then brush the steaks with the tandoori paste.

4. Put the cauliflower on an oiled baking tray and drizzle with some oil. Bake the steaks for approximately 15 minutes.

5. Set the grill to high heat setting and drizzle with a little olive oil.

6. Now cook the cauliflower steaks for an additional 2 to 3 minutes. Flip the cauliflower and cook for another 2 minutes or so.

7. At this point, mix the ingredients for the salad and stir in a bigger portion of the dressing.

8. Serve the steaks with the salad and serve with the remaining salad dressing.

Snacks and Side Dishes

Summertime Salad

Dosha Effect: Suitable for Vata, see notes if having a strong Vata imbalance. It also reduces Pitta and Kapha imbalance.

Prep Time: 15 minutes

Cook Time: 0 minutes

Total Time: 15 minutes

Serves: 2

Ingredients

1/4 cup sprouts, divided (skip for Vata)

2 cups hummus, divided

1 pinch black pepper, freshly ground

1/8 teaspoon salt

2 tablespoons fresh lemon juice or lime for Pitta

2 tablespoons olive oil

1 tablespoon sunflower seeds

1 avocado, cubed (skip for Kapha)

1/3 cup red pepper, chopped

6 cucumber slices, quartered

8 pitted and chopped kalamata olives (skip for Pitta)

6 artichoke hearts, chopped

2 cups baby spinach leafs, chopped

4 cups butter leaf or romaine lettuce, chopped

Directions

1. First, wash and chop the red pepper, cucumber, olives, artichokes, spinach and the lettuce. Put the ingredients in a mixing bowl or a large salad bowl.

2. Cube the avocado and add the cubed avocado and sunflower seeds to a large bowl.

3. Then in another bowl, add in black pepper, salt, lemon juice and olive oil. Stir the ingredients together and then pour them over the salad mix.

4. Now toss the salad until everything has been fully incorporated. Serve the salad on two large serving plates.

5. Top individual plates with a cup of the preferred hummus especially the homemade variety and then top with 1/4 cup of the sprouts.

Ayurveda Cooking Made Easy

Notes

In case you have a strong Vata imbalance such as severe anxiety, insomnia and chronic constipation, avoid the recipe and other raw foods altogether. Use the recipe and in moderation only in hotter seasons.

Ayurveda Cooking Made Easy

Sweet Lassi

Dosha Effect: Reduces Vata, Pitta and Kapha

Prep Time: 5 minutes

Cook Time: 0 minutes

Total Time: 5 minutes

Serves: 2

Ingredients

2 teaspoons honey (or maple syrup for Pitta)

1/2 teaspoon vanilla extract

3 saffron stigmas

Large pinch cardamom powder*

1/8 teaspoon ginger powder*

1/8 teaspoon turmeric*

1/4 teaspoon cinnamon*

1 cup coconut water (or water for Kapha)

1 cup plain yogurt (or non-dairy yogurt or goat yogurt or for Kapha)

Note

*You can replace the starred spices with 1/4 to 1/2 teaspoon of the Ayurvedic Breakfast Spices

Directions

1. Put coconut water and yogurt in small mixing bowl or a large jar.

2. Add in honey, vanilla, saffron, cardamom, ginger, turmeric and cinnamon and blend everything using a hand blender for 30 to 60 seconds. In case you don't have a hand blender you can use a regular blender.

3. Store the sweet lassi in an airtight container in the fridge for up to 5 days.

Doshic Variations

Pitta:

Use maple syrup in place of honey as the syrup is more cooling. Also, consider replacing store-bought yogurt with homemade yogurt as it's less sour and more cooling.

For Kapha

In place of cow yogurt, use either nondairy yogurt if possible or alternative goat yogurt. Also, replace coconut water with

Ayurveda Cooking Made Easy

plain water and double the ginger to 1/4 teaspoon along with 1 pinch of black pepper. Reduce the amount of yogurt by half in case you experience Kapha imbalance such as weight gain, cough or congestion.

Ayurveda Cooking Made Easy

Coconut Curry Hummus

Dosha Effect: Reduces Pitta and Kapha imbalance. Also increases Vata, check notes to make it friendly

Prep Time: 15 minutes

Cook Time: 0 minutes

Total Time: 15 minutes

Yields: 2 cups

Ingredients

1 can of garbanzo beans (or 1 1/2 cups cooked beans)

2 tablespoons tahini

1/2 teaspoon salt

1/8 teaspoon cayenne pepper (skip for Pitta types)

1 teaspoon cumin powder

1/2 teaspoon Agni Churna or (turmeric powder)

1/4 cup cilantro leaves, chopped

1 lime, juiced

1 tablespoon olive oil

1/4 cup raw coconut water

Directions

1. Add in fresh lime juice, olive oil and coconut water into a blender. Then chop the cilantro and add it to the blender.

2. Add in garbanzo beans, tahini, salt, cayenne pepper, cumin and turmeric to the blender.

3. Blend on high speed until the hummus is fully smooth and creamy, or for 2 to 3 minutes.

4. In case the mixture is dry, add in a little liquid and stir it halfway through. Add a little coconut water.

5. Serve the hummus as a side dish or snack, spread or a veggie dip. Store the hummus in an airtight container in your fridge for not more than 6 days.

6. To make your hummus tastier, consider cooking the beans from scratch. Just put the chickpeas in a crock-pot for about 6 to 8 hours on high heat. Then strain and use 1 1/2 cups of the chickpeas to replace the cooked beans.

Doshic Variations

Vata

Since garbanzo beans could be Vata aggravating, you might get some bloating, gas and constipation after eating. Therefore, you can choose to skip the recipe until your digestion system is restored. You can increase amounts of olive oil to 2 tablespoons if you like and replace the turmeric with Vata Churna.

Pitta:

You can omit cayenne pepper and add additional amounts of lime juice, cilantro and coconut water. Replace turmeric with Pitta Churna if possible.

Kapha:

Garbanzo beans are the best for you as they are light, airy and satiating! You may however cut the amount of tahini to 1 tablespoon and add additional cayenne pepper to boost digestion. Replace turmeric with Kapha Churna.

Steamed Veggies

Dosha Effect: Reduces Vata, Pitta and Kapha imbalance. Best for all dosha

Prep Time: 10 minutes

Cook Time: 15 minutes

Total Time: 25 minutes

Serves: 2

Ingredients

1/4 teaspoon salt

1 tablespoon ghee

1 cup chopped broccoli

1 small thinly sliced carrot

1 cup chopped cauliflower

1 medium yellow squash, chopped

1 medium zucchini, chopped

Large pinch of black pepper, freshly ground

Water, for steaming

Directions

1. Put 2 inches of water in a large pan and then put a steam basket over the water, ensuring that water level isn't above the bottom of the steam basket.

2. Set the heat to high. In case your water begins to boil even before you have chopped the veggies, reduce the heat and then cover the saucepan.

3. Now chop the broccoli, carrots, cauliflower, yellow squash and the zucchini into small bite-size chunks. The smaller the size the quicker they will cook.

4. Put the chopped vegetables into the already hot steam basket and cover the pan. You should leave a small opening to allow excess steam to escape.

5. Turn the heat to low medium and cook the chopped veggies for approximately 12 minutes.

6. As soon as 12 minutes elapse, check if the veggies are vibrant in color and are quite soft throughout.

7. In case the veggies are still hard, cover the saucepan and cook them for another 5 minutes or so, as you check them once per minute. Take care not to overcook them since they might become dull in color, flavorless and mushy.

Ayurveda Cooking Made Easy

8. If the veggies are of your preferred texture, remove the pan from heat and transfer them to a separate large bowl.

9. Now add in ghee, black pepper and salt. Stir the mixture together until the ghee coats all your vegetables.

10. Taste the veggies and then adjust the seasonings or even add extra ghee if necessary.

11. Then serve and enjoy. You can also top this on a bowl of millet, quinoa or rice.

Ayurveda Cooking Made Easy

Kale Chips

Dosha Effect: Can increase or reduce Vata. It also reduces Pitta and Kapha imbalance.

Prep Time: 15 minutes

Cook Time: 15 minutes

Total Time: 20 minutes

Serves: 2

Ingredients

1/2 lime, juiced

2 tablespoons sunflower oil

2 teaspoons Agni Churna

2 tablespoons finely ground sunflower seeds

1 bunch of kale, stemmed

Pink Himalayan salt

Pinch cayenne pepper (skip for Pitta)

Directions

1. Preheat the oven to about 300 degrees F.

Ayurveda Cooking Made Easy

2. Wash the kale and dry each individual leaf separately with paper towels. You need the kale leaves fully dry to get crispy chips. Try using a salad spinner to help save time.

3. Now cut off the stems from the kale and pull apart individual leaves into pieces measuring approximately 2x2 inches. Put the square pieces in a mixing bowl large enough to accommodate them.

4. In a blender or spice grinder grind up the sunflower seeds until you obtain a fine powder.

5. Put the ground seeds, cayenne pepper, lime juice, sunflower oil and Agni Churna into a small bowl. Stir the ingredients well until you obtain a thin paste.

6. Season the kale pieces with the sunflower seed and lime juice mixture.

7. Now rub each individual leaf with the mixture until you have covered all the kale pieces. Ensure that you apply the sauce evenly and that you don't leave any dry spots on the kale pieces.

8. Put the coated kale leaves on 2 cookie sheets, ensuring that you flatten and separate each individual kale piece so as not to overlap on each other. This helps in getting crispier kale chips.

9. Season the kale chips with some salt, just a little amount. Put the cookie sheets with the kale in your oven and set the cooking time to 7 minutes.

10. After cook time elapses, rotate the 2 cookie sheets and set the timer to another 6 minutes.

11. Check whether the kales are mildly crispy and if not just return them in the oven while checking them at 1-minute intervals until they achieve your preferred crispiness.

12. You can briefly remove the under crispy kale from the oven, let them sit for 1 minute or so before returning them to the oven to make them slightly crispier. Just ensure that the kale does not burn.

13. As soon as the kale chips are mostly crunchy and are bright green with a touch of moisture, remove the cookie sheets from the oven and let the kale chips to cool down for about 5 minutes.

14. You can now serve the kale chips and enjoy!

Note

If you are dealing with Vata imbalance, avoid this recipe as it increases Vata in excess.

Beverages

Cucumber Coconut Juice

Dosha Effect: It increases Vata and Kapha. It's also suitable for Pitta imbalance as its Pitta-reducing.

Prep Time: 15 minutes

Cook Time: 0 minutes

Total Time: 15 minutes

Serves 2

Ingredients

5 to 10 sprigs of fresh garden mint

1/2 lime

8 ounces of raw coconut water

5 apples, any variety

3 cucumbers

Directions

1. First, wash the mint, apples and cucumbers and then cut them into small pieces that can easily fit into a juicer.

2. Add the chopped ingredients to your juicer and collect the juice into a large bowl. It's recommendable to strain the juice since frothy bits may still remain in the juice.

3. Add in some coconut water and squeeze a little fresh lime juice, stir and then enjoy!

4. You can store any remaining juice in an airtight container for not more than 24 hours.

Super Greens Smoothie

Dosha Effect: *For Vata but you should avoid raw foods during Vata imbalance. It also reduces Pitta imbalance and increase Kapha.*

Prep Time: 15 minutes

Cook Time: 0 minutes

Total Time: 15 minutes

Serves 2

Ingredients

1 teaspoon coconut oil

1/2 inch cube fresh ginger

1/2 avocado

2 tablespoons goji berries, soaked in 1/2 cup of water

1 ripe peeled and chopped mango

1/2 medium ripe banana, frozen

12 ounces of water or raw coconut water

1 teaspoon Svastha Super Greens

1 teaspoon cacao nibs or raw cacao powder, skip for Vata

Directions

1. Add water to a blender and then add in the rest of the ingredients along with the water you soaked the goji berries in.

2. Blend the mixture on high-speed setting until the mixture is creamy and smooth, or for approximately 1 to 3 minutes.

3. Serve the green smoothie as a snack or for breakfast. It's advisable to eat the smoothie as a separate meal or preferably serve it after a minimum of 2 hours after eating.

Turmeric Milkshake

Dosha Effect: It reduces Vata and Pitta imbalance and increases kapha

Prep Time: 10 minutes

Cook Time: 0 minutes

Total Time: 10 minutes

Serves 2

Ingredients

1/2 teaspoon vanilla extract

1/8 teaspoon cardamom powder

1/2 to 1 teaspoon turmeric powder

1/2 to 1 teaspoon dry ginger or 1 to 2 inch cube fresh ginger, chopped

1 teaspoon cinnamon powder

3 to 4 large medjool dates without pits

1/2 of a large avocado or 1 small avocado

2 tablespoons raw pumpkin seeds, unsalted

2 tablespoons raw sunflower seeds, unsalted

2 tablespoons hemp seeds

2 tablespoons chia seeds

1 cup of raw coconut water

2 cups water

Optional extras:

1 teaspoon Shatavari powder

1 teaspoon Ashwagandha powder

Directions

1. Put everything in a high-speed blender and blend the ingredients on high setting for approximately 2 to 3 minutes.

2. Taste to test if the milkshake is smooth and creamy. In case you notice any chunks blend it for a few more seconds.

3. As soon as you achieve your preferred consistency, transfer the milkshake into a jar and tightly seal it.

4. If you have enough time, you can choose to keep the shake in the fridge or freezer for at least 1 hour. This is totally optional unless if you want cooler drink.

5. Then you can serve and enjoy.

Ayurveda Cooking Made Easy

Detox Soup

Dosha Effect: Most suitable for Kapha

Prep Time: 10 minutes

Cook Time: 5 minutes

Total Time: 15 minutes

Serves 2

Ingredients

2-4 cups water or vegetable broth

1/2 cup diced carrots

1/2 cup spinach, coarsely chopped

1 cup yellow split mung beans, cooked

1/2 cup chopped celery

1 cup leeks or onions, chopped

Salt, to taste

2 tablespoons nut paste (walnuts and pumpkin seeds)

1-2 teaspoons lemon/lime juice

1 teaspoon allspice

1/4 teaspoon cardamom powder

2 teaspoons cumin powder

A pinch of red chili flakes (if needed)

1/2-1 teaspoon black pepper, crushed

2 garlic cloves, minced

1 teaspoon fresh ginger, minced

1 tablespoon date paste

1-2 teaspoons unrefined sesame oil or olive oil

Directions

1. Add chopped veggies and oil to a stockpot and sauté together with the seasonings apart from the spinach.

2. Sauté the ingredients for approximately 5 to 10 minutes and then add in water and spinach to the mixture.

3. Now sauté for a few more minutes and then add in the mung beans. Cook until everything is well incorporated

4. Now, blend this until you achieve soup-like consistency.

5. Serve the detox soup with cubed avocados while garnished with tomatoes and parsley.

Vata-Reducing Smoothie

Dosha Effect: It reduces Vata and Pitta imbalance and increases Kapha

Prep Time: 5 minutes

Cook time: 10 minutes

Total Time: 10 minutes

Serves 2

Ingredients

2 to 3 teaspoons honey

1/2 teaspoon vanilla extract

3 saffron stigmas

1/8 teaspoon turmeric*

1/8 teaspoon cardamom*

1 teaspoon cinnamon*

1 inch cube fresh ginger, minced

1/4 cup plain yogurt

1 cup unsweetened almond milk

1 1/2 cups chopped sweet potato

*Replace the starred spices with 1 teaspoon of the Ayurvedic Breakfast Spices.

Directions

1. Put a steam basket in a medium pan and add approximately 2 inches of water into the saucepan. Ensure that the water is directly under the bottom of the basket and bring this water to a gentle boil.

2. Add the sweet potato pieces into the hot steam basket and cover the sauce pan.

3. Cook the potato over medium heat until it is soft and cooked through, or for approximately 10 to 12 minutes.

4. Meanwhile, prepare the rest of the ingredients.

5. Then add in vanilla, saffron, turmeric, cardamom, cinnamon, minced ginger, yogurt, almond milk and honey to your blender.

6. As soon as the sweet potato pieces are cooked though, add them into the blender too.

7. Blend on high speed setting for about 2 to 4 minutes.

8. You can now serve the smoothie warm topped with a little sprinkle of cinnamon.

Notes

The smoothie is best suited for winter and fall seasons to calm your mind, energize you, aid digestion and balance out Vata.

Rice Drink

Dosha Effect: Balances Vata

Prep Time: 10 minutes

Cook time: 0 minutes

Total Time: 10 minutes

Serves 2

Ingredients

2 cups warm water

¼ teaspoon ginger powder

¼ teaspoon cinnamon powder

¼ teaspoon cardamom powder

1 tablespoon ghee

2 pitted dates

1 cup cooked basmati rice

1 tablespoon maple syrup, optional

Directions

1. Blend until smooth and creamy.

Ayurveda Cooking Made Easy

2. Pour the drink in two glasses and enjoy when warm or cool at room temperature.

Avocado Shake

Dosha Effect: Balances Kapha

Prep Time 10 minutes

Total Time 10 minutes

Serves 2

Ingredients

50ml filtered, warm water

½ teaspoon vegetable stock

½ red bell pepper or capsicum

1/2 lime, juiced

1 handful spinach leaves

1 avocado

2 tomatoes

1 cucumber

Optional

Spices (turmeric, ginger, cumin)

Herbs (parsley, basil, coriander)

Extra leaves (kale, lettuce)

Directions

1. Wash everything and then chop the avocado, bell pepper, tomato and cucumber.

2. Add the vegetable stock to about 50 milliliters warm filtered water.

3. Add the vegetable stock mixture and avocado to the blender and process until you get a paste.

4. Add the ingredients that have more water content into the blender and process well.

5. Add in lime, spinach and the supplements and process until well mixed.

6. Serve and enjoy!

Conclusion

This book has given you a variety of Ayurveda recipes you can prepare and the amazing thing is that they take quite a short time to prepare; only 30 minutes; therefore, you have no excuse for preparing them.

All the best as you try out these recipes to balance your dosha.

Printed in Great Britain
by Amazon